THE LION BOOK OF

Christmas
POEMS

LION
CHILDREN'S

Written and compiled by Sophie Piper
This edition copyright © 2014 Lion Hudson

The right of the illustrators listed on p. 64 to be identified as the
illustrators of this work has been asserted by them in accordance
with the Copyright, Designs and Patents Act 1988.

Published by Lion Children's Books
an imprint of
Lion Hudson plc
Wilkinson House, Jordan Hill Road,
Oxford OX2 8DR, England
www.lionhudson.com/lionchildrens
ISBN: 978 0 7459 6510 9

First edition 2007
This edition 2014

A catalogue record for this book is available
from the British Library

Printed and bound in China, June 2014, LH07

Contents

Christmas

Christmas is prickly, shiny holly
With red berries like a robin's breast.

Christmas is big white cotton snow
Falling and falling across the world.

Christmas is red presents and warm fires,
Coming home tired with a sledge and stories.

Christmas is a place you always want to get to
And never want to leave once you're there.

Christmas is imagining turning a corner
And finding Bethlehem, the stable, the baby.

Kenneth Steven

Now the wind is coming

Now the wind is coming,
Now the wind is strong,
Now the winter freezes
And the darkness will be long.
Now we see the starlight
In the midnight sky,
We know God is with us
And the angels are close by.

The first snow

For the first time there is snow
and I simply do not know
how something quite so joyful
can fall from a frowning sky
to the sullen world below.

Does the frost-spangled wind blow
from that time so long ago
when all the world was perfect:
pure and clean and untrampled
and free from every sorrow?

Winter storms

O thought I!
What a beautiful thing
God has made winter to be
by stripping the trees
and letting us see
their shapes and forms.
What a freedom does it seem
to give to the storms.

Dorothy Wordsworth
(1771–1855)

Winter sunrise (a haiku)

Dawn of frost and grey
and then the sky fire rises
red with cheerfulness.

Winter's morning

Have you seen the frostfall
Of a winter's morning
Sparkling with white magic
In the cold blue dawning?

Christmas cat

I've built a cuddly snowcat
With whiskers made from straws –
And I'm almost sure,
I'm *almost* sure
I saw him lick his paws.

He's sitting in my garden,
He's smiling at me now,
And I'm almost sure,
I'm *almost* sure
I heard him say, 'Mee-ow!'

Clare Bevan

There was an old person of Mold

There was an old person of Mold
Who shrank from sensations of cold;
So he purchased some muffs,
Some furs and some fluffs,
And wrapped himself from the cold.

Edward Lear
(1812–1888)

I count the days to Christmas

I count the days to Christmas
and I watch the evening sky.
I want to see the angels
as to Bethlehem they fly.

I'm watching for the wise men
and the royal shining star.
Please may I travel with them?
Is the stable very far?

I count the days to Christmas
as we shop and bake and clean.
The lights and tinsel sparkle,
and yet deep inside I dream

that as we tell the story
of Lord Jesus and his birth,
the things of every day will fade
as heaven comes to earth.

15

Thoughts before Christmas

'Don't be thinking Christmas yet –
we haven't reached December.'
Well, that's what people tell me.
But why? Don't they remember
two thousand years have passed
since Jesus came down to this earth?
So I shall give my whole life long
to celebrate his birth.

Let us travel to Christmas

Let us travel to Christmas
By the light of a star.
Let us go to the hillside
Right where the shepherds are.
Let us see shining angels
Singing from heaven above.
Let us see Mary cradling
God's holy child with love.

Now light one thousand Christmas lights

Now light one thousand Christmas lights
On dark earth here tonight;
One thousand, thousand also shine
To make the dark sky bright.

Oh, once when skies were starry bright,
In a stable cold and bare,
Sweet Mary bore a son that night,
A child both kind and fair.

He came to bring us love and light
To bring us peace on earth,
So let your candles shine tonight
And sing with joy and mirth.

A traditional Swedish carol

O Christingle

O Christingle
shaped like an O
O as in Orange
O as in Glow

O as in – Oh!
What a wonderful sight
as myriads of candles
all sparkle with light.

The Chester carol

He who made the earth so fair
Slumbers in a stable bare,
Warmed by cattle standing there.

Oxen, lowing, stand all round;
In the stall no other sound
Mars the peace by Mary found.

Joseph piles the soft, sweet hay,
Starlight drives the dark away,
Angels sing a heavenly lay.

Jesu sleeps in Mary's arm;
Sheltered there from rude alarm,
None can do Him ill or harm.

See His mother o'er Him bend;
Hers the joy to soothe and tend,
Hers the bliss that knows no end.

Author unknown

21

Lucy's carol

When the Baby borned
Joseph said to Mary,
'What am I going to do about
This little-born Jesus Baby Christ?
I never knew it was going to be like
   this,
With all these angels and kings
And shepherds and stars and
   things;
It's got me worried, I can tell you,
On Christmas Day in the morning.'

Mary said to Joseph,
'Not to worry, my darling,
Dear old darling Joseph;
Everything's going to be all right,
Because the Angel told me not to fear;
So just hold up the lamp,
So I can see the dear funny sweet little face
Of my darling little-born Jesus Baby Christ.'

Joseph said to Mary,
'Behold the handyman of the Lord!'

Happy Christmas, happy Christmas!
Christ is born today.

(Lucy was five years old when she composed it;
her mother wrote it down exactly as it came)

23

The Huron carol

'Twas in the moon of wintertime when all the birds
   had fled
That mighty Gitchi Manitou sent angel choirs instead;
Before their light the stars grew dim and wandering
   hunters heard the hymn:
Jesus your King is born, Jesus is born,
   in excelsis gloria.

Within a lodge of broken bark the tender babe was
   found;
A ragged robe of rabbit skin enwrapped his beauty
   round
But as the hunter braves drew nigh, the angel song
   rang loud and high:
Jesus your King is born, Jesus is born,
   in excelsis gloria.

The earliest moon of wintertime is not so round
   and fair
As was the ring of glory on the helpless infant there.
The chiefs from far before him knelt with gifts of fox
   and beaver pelt.
Jesus your King is born, Jesus is born,
   in excelsis gloria.

O children of the forest free, O seed of Manitou,
The Holy Child of earth and heaven is born today for
  you.
Come kneel before the radiant boy who brings you
  beauty, peace and joy.
Jesus your King is born, Jesus is born,
  in excelsis gloria.

Jean de Brebeuf, around 1643;
translated by Jesse Edgar Middleton, 1926

Nativity in 20 seconds

Silent night
Candle light
Holy bright

Stable poor
Prickly straw
Donkey snore

Babe asleep
Lambs leap
Shepherds peep

Star guide
Kings ride
Manger side

Angels wing
Bells ring
Children sing
WELCOME KING!

Coral Rumble

Christmas chant

This ancient chant was sung by villagers parading through the streets early on Christmas morning.

Hail King! hail King!
Blessed is He! blessed is He!
Ho, hail! blessed the King!
Ho, hi! let there be joy!

Carmina Gadelica

Carol of the wise men

The star we've waited for so long
To tell us of his coming,
Is here! Is here! And we must go
With trumpets and drums drumming!
The star we follow on this night
Will lead us to the cradle,
Where he was born this holy night
In poor and lowly stable.

The way is long, the way is cold,
We cannot tarry longer,
The birth of him the star has told
The way is still much longer.
A king is born this holy morn
And gifts to him we're bringing.
The child we've waited for is born!
Oh hear the angels singing!

Traditional English

29

The night sky – Christmas Eve

Is this the same star
they saw from afar
Is this the same light
that shone that night
is this the same glow
that made them know
is this the same spark
that never grows dark

?

Coral Rumble

30

The wise men's story

The wise men read the skies above,
and now we read their story
of how they found the prince of peace,
newborn from heaven's glory.

We come, as if to Bethlehem,
to offer gifts of love
to make this world at Christmas time
a piece of heaven above.

Mary's song

Sleep, King Jesus,
Your royal bed
Is made of hay
In a cattle-shed.
Sleep, King Jesus,
Do not fear,
Joseph is watching
And waiting near.

Warm in the wintry air
You lie,
The ox and the donkey
Standing by,
With summer eyes
They seem to say:
Welcome, Jesus,
On Christmas Day!

Sleep, King Jesus:
Your diamond crown
   High in the sky
      Where the stars look down.
     Let your reign
       Of love begin,
         That all the world
         May enter in.

Charles Causley
(1917–2003)

The friendly beasts

Jesus our brother, kind and good,
Was humbly born in a stable rude,
And the friendly beasts around him stood;
Jesus our brother, kind and good.

'I,' said the donkey, shaggy and brown,
'I carried his mother up hill and down,
I carried her safely to Bethlehem town;
I,' said the donkey, shaggy and brown.

'I,' said the cow, all white and red,
'I gave him my manger for his bed,
I gave him my hay to pillow his head;
I,' said the cow, all white and red.

'I,' said the sheep, with the curly horn,
'I gave him my wool for his blanket warm;
He wore my coat on Christmas morn.
I,' said the sheep with the curly horn.

'I,' said the dove, from the rafters high,
'Cooed him to sleep, my mate and I,
We cooed him to sleep, my mate and I;
I,' said the dove, from the rafters high.

And every beast, by some good spell,
In the stable dark, was glad to tell,
Of the gift he gave Emmanuel,
The gift he gave Emmanuel.

Author unknown

The first mercy

Ox and ass at Bethlehem
On a night ye know of them;
We were only creatures small
Hid by shadows on the wall.

We were swallow, moth and mouse;
The Child was born in our house,
And the bright eyes of us three
Peeped at His Nativity.

Bruce Blunt

Cat in the manger

In the story, I'm not there.
Ox and ass, arranged at prayer:
But me? Nowhere.

Anti-cat evangelists
How on earth could you have missed
Such an obvious and able
Occupant of any stable?

Who excluded mouse and rat?
The harmless necessary cat.
Who snuggled in with the holy pair?
Me. And my purr.

Matthew, Mark, and Luke and John,
(Who got it wrong,
Who left out the cat)
Remember that,
Wherever He went in this great affair
I was there.

U. A. Fanthorpe

It's Christmas time

It's Christmas time,
When angels come
To earth from heaven above.
Take a golden gift box
And fill it full of love.

It's Christmas time!
The angels' song
Is heard upon the ground.
Open up the gift box,
Let love shine all around.

A golden string

I give you the end of a golden string;
Only wind it into a ball:
It will lead you in at Heaven's gate,
Built in Jerusalem's wall.

William Blake
(1757–1827)

39

I will choose a Christmas tree

I will choose a Christmas tree
to celebrate the Birth:
I will plant it carefully
upon God's good deep earth.

I will tend my Christmas tree
in honour of the Child:
I will leave it growing
in the wetness and the wild.

A bunch of holly

But give me holly, bold and jolly,
Honest, prickly, shining holly;
Pluck me holly leaf and berry
For the day when I make merry.

Christina Rossetti
(1830–1894)

Shop till you drop

'Shop till you drop this Christmas.'
Well, that's what everyone said.
Is that 'till you drop the parcels',
or else 'till you drop down dead'?

'Eat all you can this Christmas,
yes, eat till you're fit to burst.'
Is that 'till you burst a button',
or do they mean something worse?

'Do a good deed this Christmas.'
That's a more interesting one.
Is that to say thanks for the
presents
or 'do good to
everyone'?

Christmas for free

Christmas is expensive, my grandma said to me,
Except for Christmas starlight – that shines on
   earth for free,
And frost like silver tinsel on every woodland tree
And all the love that we can share together,
   you and me.

Night drive

Mum and Dad make a bed for me in the back.
The car is cosy and I creep under the rugs
Not quite wanting to go to sleep,
Listening to their voices softly talking.

And I want to get there and yet I don't;
When I rub my hand against the steamed-up window
I see stars and the lights of distant farms,
And I think of the children lying there asleep.

We drive up and up on a windy road,
I can see snowflakes blink against the window.
An owl comes out of the dark like a ghost,
And I catch a glimpse of its round white face.

We reach home in the end and I am carried inside
(It is all so strange in the middle of the night)
I drink hot cocoa and snuggle into bed,
And I dream of the night drive until morning.

Kenneth Steven

I thought I saw
a wintry branch

I thought I saw a wintry branch
against a wintry sky;
I looked again and saw it was
a reindeer prancing by.

I thought I saw the setting sun
melt into gold and red;
I looked again and saw it was
Old Santa in his sled.

Christmas lights

The Christmas lights are flashing
in gold and red and green
but, clear above, the starlight
is silver and serene.

Christmas presents

I really love Christmas Eve
when we put the presents
under the tree:
a gleeful heap
of promises
in red and green
gold and silver
tags and ribbons
and loads and loads
of love.

And then, on
Christmas Day,
there are splendid
things to see:
gadgets and gizmos
toys and socks
nuts and chocolates
and foaming bath perfumes in
exotic bottles.
But somehow the
magic has gone.

Inside I know
that what I really wanted
(although it wasn't on my list)
was for all the gift-wrapped promises
   to come true
for all the parcels to spill over
not with shredded tissue paper
but with joyful love and happy laughter
and to be able to reach down and find…

Christmas!

What do you want for Christmas?

'For Christmas, would you like some gold?'
I'd rather just have money.
'And what about some frankincense?'
Come on, you're being funny.

And what is more, I don't want… 'No!
I've gone and bought the myrrh!'
*You could have asked me for a list
of things that I'd prefer.*

'You're not exactly Jesus then?'
*Oh, no. I'm plain old me.
And I want fairly normal gifts
left underneath the tree:*

I'll have this season's latest fad,
to be like all my friends
And chocolate that will last me, oh,
at least till this year ends.

'But Christmas gifts should be much more –
they should have lasting worth.'
May I suggest good will to all
and maybe peace on earth.

I know the Santa

I know the Santa whose feet I heard creep
I know the sandman who sends me to sleep
I know the reindeer who walks on my roof
I know the fairy who found my front tooth.

I know the green elf who makes all my toys
I know the monster who makes all that noise
I know the birdie who sees what I do
I know them all, and they all look like you.

Steve Turner

A letter from Santa

Dear Boys and Girls,

Ho ho ho! You have been good.

You hung up your stockings very neatly and it was easy to find and fill them.

I found a note alongside my plate of goodies (thank you) asking me to ask you if you would like to try hanging up all your clothes all year round.

It might have been your mother's handwriting.

See you next year... if you're very good.

Santa

Christmas morning

Frost white morning
Very Crisp-mas.

All the aunties
Scary Kiss-mas.

Fun and laughter
Merry Christmas!

Christmas mice

No Christmas mouse
inside our house –
we're much too neat
for that.

Our gift to mice
at Christmas is
their natural
habitat.

All in tune

All in tune to William's flute
Now is Robin's tabor,
Dance tonight and sing high praise
As they did in other days,
Every kindly neighbour.
All in tune, all in tune,
Are the flute and tambourine,
All in tune, all in tune,
Heaven and earth tonight are seen.

God and man are in accord,
More than flute or tabor,
Dance for joy and sing with awe,
For the child upon the straw
Is our God and neighbour.
God and man, God and man,
Are like flute and tambourine,
God and man, God and man,
As true neighbours here are seen.

Anonymous

The road to Bethlehem

Hard is the road to Bethlehem
Love is a hard, hard road.

Winding the road to Bethlehem
Joy is a winding road.

Long is the road to Bethlehem
Peace is a long, long road.

The prayer of St Francis

Lord, make me an instrument of your peace.
Where there is hatred, let me sow love;
Where there is injury, pardon;
Where there is discord, union;
Where there is doubt, faith;
Where there is despair, hope;
Where there is darkness, light;
Where there is sadness, joy;
For your mercy and your truth's sake.

Attributed to St Francis of Assisi
(1181–1226)

Heaven on earth

Somehow, not only for Christmas,
But all the long year through,
The joy that you give to others,
Is the joy that comes back to you.
And the more you spend in blessing
The poor and lonely and sad,
The more of your heart's possessing
Returns to you glad.

John Greenleaf Whittier
(1807–92)

Hope

Hope is the thing with feathers
That perches in the soul,
And sings the tune without the words
And never stops at all,

And sweetest in the gale is heard;
And sore must be the storm
That could abash the little bird
That kept so many warm.

I've heard it in the chillest land,
And on the strangest sea;
Yet, never, in extremity,
It asked a crumb of me.

Emily Dickinson
(1830–86)

A Christmas blessing

God bless the master of this house,
The mistress also,
And all the little children
That round the table go;
And all your kin and kinsfolk,
That dwell both far and near:
I wish you a Merry Christmas
And a Happy New Year.

Author unknown

Angel of God

Angel of God, my guardian dear
To whom God's love commits me here,
Ever this day be at my side
To light and guard, to rule and guide.

Traditional

Come again

Noël is leaving us,
Sad 'tis to tell,
But he will come again,
Goodbye, Noël.
The kings ride away
In the snow and the rain,
After twelve months
We shall see them again.

Traditional French

Acknowledgments

Every effort has been made to trace and contact copyright owners. We apologize for any inadvertent omissions or errors.

Poems

pp. 7, 8, 10, 11, 14, 16, 17, 18, 31, 38, 42, 43, 48, 50 by Lois Rock; pp. 19, 40, 46, 47, 53, 54 (both), 58 by Sophie Piper. Copyright © Lion Hudson.

p.6 'Christmas' and p.44 'Night drive' taken from *Imagining Things* by Kenneth Steven, Lion Children's Books (2005). Copyright © Kenneth Steven. Used with permission of the author.

p.12 'Christmas cat' by Clare Bevan taken from *Christmas Poems* chosen by Fiona Waters, Macmillan (2006). Copyright © 2006 Clare Bevan. Used with permission of the author.

p.22 'Lucy's carol' taken from *A Pocket Book of Spiritual Poems* collected by Rumer Godden, Hodder and Stoughton Ltd (1996).

p.26 'Nativity in 20 seconds' and p.30 'The night sky – Christmas Eve' taken from *Breaking the Rules* by Coral Rumble, Lion Children's Books (2004). Copyright © 2004 Coral Rumble. Used with permission of the author.

p.32 'Mary's song' from *Collected Poems for Children* by Charles Causley, Macmillan. Used with permission of David Higham Associates Ltd.

p.34 'The friendly beasts' taken from *Poems for Christmas* compiled by Zenka and Ian Woodward, Hutchinson Children's Books (1984).

p.37 'Cat in the manger' taken from *Christmas Poems* by U.A. Fanthorpe, Enitharmon/Peterloo Poets (2002). Copyright © 2002 U.A. Fanthorpe. Used with permission of Peterloo Poets and the author.

p.52 'I know the Santa' taken from *The Day I Fell Down the Toilet* by Steve Turner, Lion Children's Books (1996). Copyright © 1996 Steve Turner. Used with permission of the author.

Carmina Gadelica collected by Alexander Carmichael is published by Floris Books, Edinburgh.

Illustrations

Copyright © Sheila Moxley: pp. 1, 2, 3, 4, 14–15, 16–17, 26–27, 44–45, 56–57 and the cover. Copyright © Debbie Lush: pp. 3, 6–7. Copyright © Elena Temporin: pp. 4, 20–21, 38–39, 60–61. Copyright © Ruth Rivers: pp. 4, 10–11, 42–43, 46–47. Copyright © Christina Balit: pp. 4, 24–25, 28–29, 30–31. Copyright © Liz Pichon: pp. 12, 40–41, 52–53, 54–55. Copyright © Helen Cann: pp. 22–23, 36–37. Copyright © Julie Downing: pp. 5, 32–33, 35, 48–49, 58–59, 63. Copyright © Sarah Young: pp. 50–51. Photographs on pages 3 and 18–19 by John Williams.